MW00975371

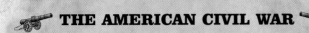

THE AMERICAN CIVIL WAR

FAMOUS CONFEDERATE GENERALS AND LEADERS OF THE SOUTH

A MyReportLinks.com Book

Pat McCarthy

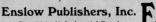

MyReportLinks.com Books

an imprint of

Enslow Publishers, Inc. **E**

Box 398, 40 Industrial Road
Berkeley Heights, NJ 07922
USA

YEOKUM MEDIA CENTER
BELTON, MO.
WITHDRAWN

MyReportLinks.com Books, an imprint of Enslow Publishers, Inc. MyReportLinks®
is a registered trademark of Enslow Publishers, Inc.

Copyright © 2004 by Enslow Publishers, Inc.

All rights reserved.

No part of this book may be reproduced by any means
without the written permission of the publisher.

Library of Congress Cataloging-in-Publication Data

McCarthy, Pat, 1940–
  Famous Confederate generals and leaders of the South: a
myreportlinks.com book / Pat McCarthy.
    p. cm. — (The American civil war)
  Includes bibliographical references (p.   ) and index.
  ISBN 0-7660-5189-7
Generals—Confederate States of America—Biography—Juvenile
literature. 2. Politicians—Confederate States of America—Biography—
Juvenile literature. 3. United States—History—Civil War, 1861–1865—
Biography—Juvenile literature. 4. Confederate States of America—
Biography—Juvenile literature. 5. Confederate States of America—Politics
and government—Juvenile literature. I. Title. II. Series.
E467.M39 2004
973.7'42'0922—dc22

                              2004000095

Printed in the United States of America

10 9 8 7 6 5 4 3 2 1

To Our Readers:
Through the purchase of this book, you and your library gain access to the Report Links that specifically back up this book.

The Publisher will provide access to the Report Links that back up this book and will keep these Report Links up to date on **www.myreportlinks.com** for three years from the book's first publication date.

We have done our best to make sure all Internet addresses in this book were active and appropriate when we went to press. However, the author and the Publisher have no control over, and assume no liability for, the material available on those Internet sites or on other Web sites they may link to.

The usage of the MyReportLinks.com Books Web site is subject to the terms and conditions stated on the Usage Policy Statement on **www.myreportlinks.com**.

A password may be required to access the Report Links that back up this book. The password is found on the bottom of page 4 of this book.

Any comments or suggestions can be sent by e-mail to comments@myreportlinks.com or to the address on the back cover.

Photo Credits: © Hemera Technologies, Inc., 1997–2001, p. 9 (flags); Civil War Homepage, pp. 25, 27; Gilder Lehrman Institute of American History/The Chicago Historical Society, p. 31; Library of Congress, pp. 1, 3, 10, 12, 13, 17, 18, 22, 29, 33, 36, 44; MyReportLinks.com Books, pp. 4, back cover; Smithsonian Institution, p. 38; The American Civil War, p. 40; The History Place, pp. 35, 42; Tulane University, p. 15.

Cover Photos: Images of Jefferson Davis, Robert E. Lee, Stonewall Jackson, and Battle of First Manassas, Library of Congress.

Contents

Report Links **4**

**Famous Generals and Leaders
of the South Facts** **9**

1 Lee's Great Decision **10**

2 The Southern Perspective **13**

**3 The Political Leaders of
the Confederacy** **17**

4 The Confederacy's Leading Generals **29**

Chapter Notes **46**

Further Reading **47**

Index **48**

MyReportLinks.com Books
Great Books, Great Links, Great for Research!

The Report Links listed on the following four pages can save you hours of research time by **instantly** bringing you to the best Web sites relating to your report topic.

How to Use MyReportLinks.com

1 Got a Report to do?

2 Check out a MyReportLinks.com Book at the Library.

3 Read the Book.

4 Go to www.myreportlinks.com for Quick, Safe, and Up-to-Date Links!

5 Internet Report Links = Great Information.

6 Write Your Report. Impress Your Teacher.

MAX LYNX

The pre-evaluated Web sites are your links to source documents, photographs, illustrations, and maps. They also provide links to dozens—even hundreds—of Web sites about your report subject.

MyReportLinks.com Books and the MyReportLinks.com Web site save you time and make report writing easier than ever!

Please see "To Our Readers" on the copyright page for important information about this book, the MyReportLinks.com Web site, and the Report Links that back up this book. Please enter **WES4774** if asked for a password.

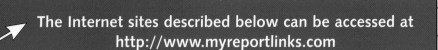
The Internet sites described below can be accessed at
http://www.myreportlinks.com

▶**Southern Leaders**　　　　　　　　　　　　　　*EDITOR'S CHOICE
This site provides biographies on Confederate leaders including Robert
E. Lee, Jefferson Davis, James Longstreet, Stonewall Jackson, and more.

▶**Jefferson Davis**　　　　　　　　　　　　　　*EDITOR'S CHOICE
This Web site provides a brief biography of Jefferson Davis, who served
as the president of the Confederate States of America.

▶**Robert E. Lee (1–19–1807 / 10–12–1870)**　　*EDITOR'S CHOICE
On this Web site you can read a biography of the man generally
considered to be the Confederacy's greatest general, Robert E. Lee.

▶**The History Place: A Nation Divided—**
The U.S. Civil War 1861–1865　　　　　　　*EDITOR'S CHOICE
This Web site provides a time line of the major events that took place
during the American Civil War, 1861 to 1865.

▶**The American Civil War Homepage**　　　　　*EDITOR'S CHOICE
Here you will find an organized list of online Civil War resources.
Biographies, military facts, images, documents, and other information
are included.

▶**Virginia Military Institute Archives:**
Stonewall Jackson Resources　　　　　　　*EDITOR'S CHOICE
This site from the Virginia Military Institute contains General Thomas
J. "Stonewall" Jackson's biography, the complete text of his letters, and
other resources. Jackson taught at the institute before the Civil War.

Report Links

The Internet sites described below can be accessed at http://www.myreportlinks.com

▶**Albert S. Johnston**

On this site you can read a brief biography of the highly esteemed Confederate general Albert Sidney Johnston, who was killed in the Battle of Shiloh.

▶**Alexander H. Stephens**

Alexander H. Stephens was a United States congressman and later served as the vice president of the Confederacy. A brief biography of Stephens is included in this site.

▶**The Apotheosis of Robert E. Lee**

This University of Virginia site examines the cultural legacy of Robert E. Lee as a Virginian, a Southerner, and an American. Art and literature are the focus.

▶**The Civil War**

This PBS site contains a wide range of information about the Civil War. Biographies of important figures, maps, historical documents, and other resources are included.

▶**Civil War and Reconstruction, 1861–1877: The South During the Civil War**

Documents from this Library of Congress site show how the Civil War affected the people living in the South.

▶**The Compromise of 1850 and the Fugitive Slave Act**

The Compromise of 1850 briefly smoothed over differences between the North and South on issues of new territories and slavery. Here you will find a brief description of the compromise.

▶**Crisis at Fort Sumter**

This Tulane University site offers an in-depth look at the crisis at Fort Sumter, where the opening shots of the Civil War were fired. The causes and effects of the conflict are examined here.

▶**Documenting the American South**

This archival site from the University of North Carolina at Chapel Hill presents first-person narratives of ordinary Southerners from colonial times through the early twentieth century.

Any comments? Contact us: **comments@myreportlinks.com**

Report Links

The Internet sites described below can be accessed at http://www.myreportlinks.com

▶**Emancipation Proclamation**
The Emancipation Proclamation, which freed slaves in the states under rebellion, was issued by President Lincoln during the Civil War. Here you will find the history and drafts of the document.

▶**Francis P. Blair**
Francis P. Blair was an important figure in American politics for over half a century. Here you will find his brief biography.

▶**A House Divided: America in the Age of Lincoln**
This online exhibit focuses on American culture during Abraham Lincoln's life. Issues of slavery and the Civil War are covered in depth.

▶**James Ewell Brown Stuart (1833–1864)**
General James E. B. "Jeb" Stuart was a key figure in capturing John Brown at the raid on Harpers Ferry and a fearless Confederate general during the Civil War. This site features a biography of Stuart.

▶**James Longstreet**
An interesting and sympathetic account of the life and Civil War action of General James Longstreet is featured in this site.

▶**John Slidell (1793–1871)**
John Slidell, a Northerner who moved to Louisiana and served as a diplomat to France for the Confederacy, is profiled in this site.

▶**Joseph E. Johnston**
Joseph E. Johnston was a veteran of the Seminole Wars and the Mexican-American War by the time he participated in the Civil War. This site includes a biography of the Confederate general.

▶**Judah Benjamin, the Jewish Confederate**
Judah P. Benjamin served as the attorney general, secretary of war, and secretary of state for the Confederacy. Read a brief biography of him on this site.

The Internet sites described below can be accessed at
http://www.myreportlinks.com

▶**Leaders**

On this Web site from the Smithsonian Institution, you can view a collection of portraits of Civil War leaders from both the Confederacy and the Union.

▶**National Park Service: Learn About Slavery**

This National Park Service site discusses the history of slavery in America. Here you will find information about maroon societies, slave rebellions, opposition to slavery, the Civil War, and emancipation.

▶**The Papers of Jefferson Davis**

This comprehensive site from Rice University contains the papers of Jefferson Davis. Biographical information on the president of the Confederacy is included as well.

▶**Pierre Gustave Toutant Beauregard (1818–1893)**

This site provides a brief biography of Confederate general Pierre Gustave Toutant Beauregard, who commanded the Confederate troops that fired on Fort Sumter.

▶**Slavery in America**

This site contains a vast amount of information on the history of slavery in the United States. The literature of slavery, slave narratives, and links to other sites are included.

▶**The Time of the Lincolns**

This PBS site is dedicated to American life during the time of Abraham and Mary Todd Lincoln. Topics such as politics, social issues, and the Civil War are included.

▶**The *Trent* Affair**

The *Trent* Affair, which involved Confederate diplomats aboard a British ship that was stopped by a Union vessel, nearly brought Great Britain into the American Civil War. This site features a history of the event.

▶**What Caused the Civil War?**

This Gettysburg National Military Park article is an overview of the causes of the Civil War. Tariffs, sectionalism, states' rights, slavery, and other factors are discussed here.

Famous Generals and Leaders of the South Facts

Robert Edward Lee Born Westmoreland County, Virginia, 1807; died 1870. General, adviser to Jefferson Davis; commanded Army of Northern Virginia; appointed general-in-chief of all Confederate armies, 1865; president, Washington College (now Washington and Lee University), 1865–1870.

Thomas Jonathan "Stonewall" Jackson Born Clarksburg, Virginia (now West Virginia), 1824; died 1863. General who earned the nickname "Stonewall" at the First Battle of Manassas, 1861; led Shenandoah Valley campaign and served Lee well in Seven Days' Battles.

James Longstreet Born Edgefield District, South Carolina, 1821; died 1904. General who commanded troops at Second Manassas, Antietam, Gettysburg, Chickamauga; often blamed for delay that led to Confederate defeat at Gettysburg; surrendered with Lee at Appomattox.

James Ewell Brown (Jeb) Stuart Born Patrick County, Virginia, 1833; died 1864. General who distinguished himself at First Manassas and led raids around McClellan's army; commanded Confederate right wing at Fredericksburg; defeated and mortally wounded at Spotsylvania, 1864.

Albert Sidney Johnston Born Washington, Kentucky, 1803; died 1862. General considered by Jefferson Davis as one of his best; led Confederate victory at Shiloh, 1862, but was mortally wounded there.

Joseph Eggleston Johnston Born near Farmville, Virginia, 1807; died 1891. General in command of Army of Northern Virginia, 1861–1862; defeated by Grant at Vicksburg, 1863; surrendered to Sherman, 1865.

Jefferson Davis Born Fairview, Kentucky, 1808; died 1889. Served in U.S. House of Representatives and Senate before resigning when Mississippi seceded; served as president of the Confederate States of America, 1861–1865; indicted for treason, 1866, but never prosecuted.

Alexander Hamilton Stephens Born Wilkes County, Georgia, 1812; died 1883. Served in U.S. House of Representatives, 1843–1859; vice president of the Confederacy, 1861–1865; imprisoned in Boston following end of war; member U.S. House of Representatives, 1873–1882; governor of Georgia, 1883.

Judah Philip Benjamin Born St. Croix, Virgin Islands, 1811; died 1884. Served as U.S. senator from Louisiana, 1853–1861; served as attorney general, secretary of war, and secretary of state of the Confederacy; escaped to England following Confederate defeat.

John Slidell Born New York City, 1793; died 1871. Member U.S. House of Representatives, 1843–1845, and U.S. Senate, 1853–1861; resigned from Senate to join Confederacy in 1861; appointed as diplomat to France for the Confederate States of America, 1861; involved in the *Trent* Affair, 1861; failed in efforts to have France recognize the Confederacy.

Chapter 1

Lee's Great Decision

Robert Edward Lee was asked to serve as general-in-chief of the United States Army when the Civil War began. Winfield Scott had held that position since 1841. However, he was too old for active field command by 1861.

Lee had served under Scott in the Mexican-American War (1846–48), and Scott had been impressed with him. In fact, Scott once suggested that if there were another war, the government should insure Lee's life for $5 million. Lee had learned a great deal from Scott, who taught him to make maximum use of his army so he would be able to defeat a larger force. Scott taught Lee to maneuver, to act decisively, and to use reconnaissance information to map out his strategy. Lee would use all these skills in the Civil War, but they would not be used as Scott had intended them to be.

◀ Robert E. Lee's decision to fight for the Confederacy was an extremely difficult one for the man who had once been superintendent of the United States Military Academy at West Point.

Lee had proved to be an outstanding officer in Mexico, so it was only natural that Scott hoped Lee would take his place. On February 13, 1861, Lee received orders to report to Winfield Scott in Washington. Earlier that month, seven seceded Southern states had met to form a new nation: the Confederate States of America. When Lee arrived in Washington, Francis P. Blair, a close friend and adviser to President Abraham Lincoln, offered Lee command of the United States Army. Lee, however, refused. As a Virginian and a Southerner, he felt he could not make war against his own people even though Virginia at the time remained in the Union.

It did not remain in the Union for long. On April 17, less than a week after the opening shots of the Civil War were fired, Virginia voted to secede. On April 19, Lee wrote a letter to Scott, thanking him for all he had done for him and informing him that he was resigning his commission. "I shall carry to the grave the most grateful recollections of your kind consideration," he wrote, "and your name and fame will always be dear to me."[1]

Lee wrote another letter the same night, informing Secretary of War Simon Cameron of his decision to resign his commission in the United States Army. Two days later, Virginia governor John Letcher sent Lee a message that he wanted to talk to him the next day in Richmond. Lee went to the Confederate capital, and there Letcher asked him to accept command of "the military and naval forces of Virginia."[2] Lee accepted and was given the rank of major general.

Robert E. Lee believed the South had been mistreated by the North in many ways, but he did not believe that secession was necessary, and he hoped that the divisions

between the North and the South could be settled in a peaceful manner. He had said he would sacrifice anything except honor to preserve the Union, and it was, in the end, honor and loyalty that kept him from deserting his family and friends in Virginia. But his decision had been a difficult one. He wrote to his sister, "With all my devotion to the Union, and the feeling of loyalty and duty of an American citizen, I have not been able to make up my mind to raise my hand against my relatives, my children, my home."[3]

Painful though it had been, Lee made the decision, in spite of the conflicts between his beliefs and his feelings, to serve the Confederacy in the bloodiest war in United States history—the American Civil War.

◀ *Opposed to secession and war, Robert Edward Lee, a son of Virginia, was also opposed to what he considered "an invasion of the Southern States."*

The Southern Perspective

The first shots of the Civil War were fired by Confederate guns at Fort Sumter, South Carolina, in April 1861. Fort Sumter was a federal fort, but when South Carolina seceded, or left, the United States of America in December of the preceding year, it claimed that all of the

Africans in America/Part 4/ Close-up - Microsoft Internet Explorer

File   Edit   View   Favorites   Tools   Help

Address http://www.pbs.org/wgbh/aia/part4/4h1565b.html   Go

Internet

▲ Slaves from the plantation of James Joyner Smith, in Beaufort, South Carolina, are pictured after Joyner and fellow slaveholders fled their plantations once Union troops entered the area in 1861.

YEOKUM MEDIA CENTER
BELTON, MO.

federal forts within its lands were no longer the property of the United States. The tensions between North and South that led to the first shots at Fort Sumter, however, had been mounting since the founding of the nation, and those tensions revolved around the question of slavery.

North vs. South

Since America's earliest days, the North and the South were very different in many ways. The economy of the South was more dependent on agriculture than that of the North. Agriculture was important to the North, but the North had a more diversified economy than the South. Wealthy Southern planters knew that their whole way of life depended on slavery, since the owners of large cotton plantations depended almost solely on slave labor.

Southerners believed that slavery was less widespread in the North not because of any great humanitarian feelings on the part of Northerners, but because slavery did not serve a practical purpose there. Even though only a small percentage of Southerners owned slaves, those Southerners held the most power.

The Union and States' Rights

The South also differed from the North on its interpretation of the Union. Southerners believed that the Union had been formed by the consent of the governed, not by force, and therefore they did not think that force should be used to keep the Union intact. Southern politicians thought that if some of those who had agreed to be part of the Union no longer believed that the Union served them well, they should have the authority to leave the Union peacefully.

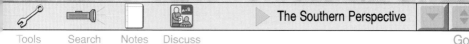
While Northerners generally believed in a strong federal government that took precedence over the wishes of the individual states, Southerners believed strongly in states' rights. They claimed that the source of political authority lay with the separate states, not with the Union. Most Southerners had a stronger sense of loyalty to their individual states than they did to the Union.

They based their claims on the Tenth Amendment to the United States Constitution, which says, "The Powers not designated to the United States by the Constitution, nor prohibited by it to the States, are reserved to the States respectively, or to the people."[1]

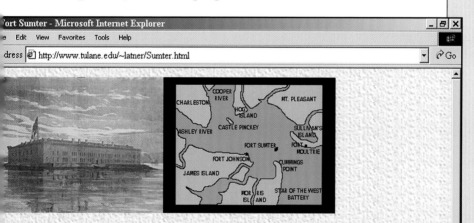

Fort Sumter - Microsoft Internet Explorer

Edit   View   Favorites   Tools   Help

dress   http://www.tulane.edu/~latner/Sumter.html   Go

ort Sumter

rt Sumter, named after a South Carolina Revolutionary War hero, was designed as part of lefensive system for Charleston Harbor. Plans were drawn in 1827, and construction gan two years later. Located on a man-made island of sea shells and grani te from rthern quarries, it was a pentagonal structure, fifty feet high, with walls eight to twelve et thick.

one   Internet

△ The first shots of the Civil War were fired upon Fort Sumter, in Charleston Harbor. South Carolina had been the first state to secede from the Union, and now it was the site of the war's first battle.

Southerners also protested against tariffs—taxes on imported goods—that benefited the more industrial North but were considered harmful to Southern interests. South Carolina, the first state to secede from the Union, had threatened to do so as early as 1832 over a tariff it considered to be unconstitutional.

Secession and War

Over the nineteenth century, the population of the North grew much faster than that of the South. Immigrants usually settled in the North, where they could get jobs in industry. By 1850, two thirds of the people in the United States lived in the North. The South was worried that they would be swallowed up by the North. Southerners believed that they were not fairly represented in Congress and they were not being treated fairly by the federal government. From there it was a short step to the idea of seceding from the Union. When Abraham Lincoln, a Republican and opponent of the expansion of slavery, was elected president of the United States in November 1860, South Carolina seceded the following month, followed in the next six months by ten other Southern states. These eleven states formed the Confederate States of America.

It seemed logical to the leaders of the South that they would be better off with their own nation. They would not have to deal with the differences they had with the North, and they saw no reason why the two countries could not coexist peacefully. When it was clear that the North would not surrender its federal forts that lay in Confederate lands—like Fort Sumter, in Charleston, South Carolina—that peaceful coexistence ended, and the Civil War began.

Chapter 3 ▶

The Political Leaders of the Confederacy

As president of the Confederate States of America, Jefferson Davis served as the political leader of the Confederacy. Davis had been opposed to secession even after South Carolina seceded from the Union in December 1860.

The tenth and final child in his family, Davis was born in Kentucky in 1808. His family moved to Mississippi, where he was educated at home for a time before being sent to a boarding school in Kentucky. He entered Transylvania University in Lexington when he was fourteen. He did well there, studying ancient languages, history, and science. Davis was well liked at Transylvania. George W. Jones, who later became a senator from Iowa, recalled that Davis "was the most intelligent and best loved student in the University."[1]

◀ *Jefferson Davis, the president of the Confederate States of America, was born in Kentucky not far from the birthplace of another president—Abraham Lincoln.*

Davis was appointed to the United States Military Academy at West Point by President James Monroe. A classmate there said of Davis, "He was distinguished in his corps for manly bearing and high-toned and lofty character."[2] Davis graduated in June 1828 at the age of twenty. His first active service was in the Old Northwest where he participated in military action against Sauk and Fox Indians in the Black Hawk War. Davis was put in charge of Chief Black Hawk when he was captured, and the Sauk

Davis was inaugurated the president of the Confederate States of America on February 22, 1862, in Richmond, the Confederate capital.

and Fox chief talked about the kind treatment he received from the young officer.

Davis remained in the service until 1835, when he surprised everyone by resigning to become a cotton planter. He married Sallie Knox Taylor, daughter of Zachary Taylor, former United States president, who disapproved of the marriage. Unfortunately, three months later, both Davis and his wife contracted malaria, and his wife, known as Knox, died from the disease. Davis recovered but was devastated. Ten years later, Davis remarried. His second wife, Varina Howell, was seventeen years younger than Davis.

Davis became interested in politics and was elected to Congress as a representative from Mississippi in 1845. In his speeches, he showed devotion to the Union but remained an advocate of states' rights.

Davis resigned his seat in Congress in June 1846 and rejoined the military. He served with a regiment in New Orleans and served with his former father-in-law, Zachary Taylor. He and his Mississippi regiment fought admirably in the Mexican-American War, and Taylor in his report mentioned Davis's courage, coolness, and successful service. Davis had been wounded in the last battle of the war but had remained on the battlefield till victory was won.

In 1847, the governor of Mississippi appointed Jefferson Davis to fill a vacancy in the United States Senate that was brought about by the death of Senator Jesse Speight. Davis was later elected for a full term, and he soon became known as a leader in the South's fight to uphold states' rights and slavery.

Davis did not approve of the Compromise of 1850, which admitted California to the Union as a free state while organizing the territories that had been gained by

the United States following its victory over Mexico. To satisfy the Southern states, a strong Fugitive Slave Law was attached to the compromise, requiring citizens to aid in the recovery of runaway slaves and making it a federal crime to assist fugitive slaves.

Despite this tough new law, Davis did not consider the Compromise of 1850 favorable to the South, but he also did not agree with those who talked of breaking up the Union. He later said, "My devotion to the Union of our fathers had been so often and so publicly declared. . . . I regarded the separation of the States as a great, though not the greater, evil."[3]

In 1852, Franklin Pierce was elected president of the United States and asked Jefferson Davis to join his cabinet as secretary of war. After first turning down the position, Davis finally accepted. In 1857, Davis was again elected to the Senate, where he remained until Mississippi seceded from the Union on January 9, 1861. In February, the provisional Congress of the Confederate States of America named him president of the Confederacy. Later that year, he was elected to a six-year term as president by popular vote and inaugurated early in 1862.

In his inaugural address, Davis stated that the Confederacy "illustrates the American idea that governments rest upon the consent of the governed, and that it is the right of the people to alter or abolish governments whenever they become destructive of the ends for which they were established."[4]

In many ways, Davis was a failure as the president of the Confederacy. He failed to raise enough money to fight the war. He was also unable to get recognition or help from foreign governments, which would have greatly aided the Confederate cause. Davis believed that he

 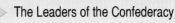

ttp://www.historyplace.com/civilwar/cwar-pix/confed-whouse.jpg - Microsoft Internet Explorer

Edit   View   Favorites   Tools   Help

dress http://www.historyplace.com/civilwar/cwar-pix/confed-whouse.jpg   Go

Internet

The Confederate White House in Richmond served as the executive mansion for Jefferson Davis and his family from August 1861 to the end of the war in 1865. It was also the political and military center of the Confederacy. It is now a National Historic Landmark.

should appoint high military officials, and the governors of the states disagreed. He often clashed with his generals because he wanted to plan their strategies for them.

Davis did succeed in raising a formidable army that was able to defend itself against a much larger Union force. He also encouraged industry in the South. Even in 1865, he maintained his belief in the Confederacy and believed his forces would be able to win the war.

When the war ended in 1865, Jefferson Davis was captured by federal troops and was imprisoned for

treason, but he was never prosecuted and was released in 1867. The following year, the federal government (led by President Andrew Johnson, a Southerner) dropped its charges against Davis.

Davis's last years were spent in several unsuccessful business ventures, although he did write an account of the Confederacy titled *The Rise and Fall of the Confederate Government*. He died in New Orleans in 1889.

Alexander Hamilton Stephens

Like Jefferson Davis, Alexander Hamilton Stephens did not want the Southern states to secede from the Union when they did. However, unlike Davis, Stephens believed secession was legal—he just did not think its time had come. When the time came, Stephens was named vice president of the Confederacy, serving under Jefferson Davis.

Stephens, born in Georgia, went to college and then became a lawyer. He did not spend much time practicing law, however. Two years after he was admitted to the bar, he

Alexander Stephens cast his vote against secession when Georgia voted to secede from the Union. But he accepted his state's decision and became a delegate to the February 1861 convention held in Montgomery, Alabama, where the Confederacy was born.

was elected to the Georgia state legislature. He served until 1841, when he declined reelection. The next year, though, he was chosen as a state senator.

Stephens moved from the Georgia state legislature to the United States Congress as a representative from Georgia in 1843. He served there for sixteen years and then returned to private life in 1859. Like many Southern politicians, Stephens was alarmed when Abraham Lincoln was elected president in 1860, but he initially worked to keep Georgia from seceding.

When his efforts failed and Georgia did secede on January 19, 1861, Stephens threw all his energies into supporting the Confederacy. He was named to the Provisional Congress, which met in Montgomery, Alabama, the Confederacy's first capital, in February 1861. Alexander Stephens had hoped to be named president of the provisional government, but Jefferson Davis earned that honor instead.

As time went on, Davis consulted Stephens less and less on the political matters of the Confederacy, and Davis did not consider Stephens qualified as an adviser on military affairs. Stephens, a proud and sensitive man, grew more and more resentful of the Confederacy's president.

In the spring of 1864, Stephens wrote Davis a long letter that stated his views on how the Confederacy should fight the war. Stephens also made a speech to the Georgia legislature in which he denounced the Davis administration, calling it tyranny. Stephens's repeated criticisms of Davis continued to irritate the Confederate president. However, in January 1865, Davis sent Stephens, along with John A. Campbell and Robert M. T. Hunter, to meet informally with Abraham Lincoln. They met on a steamer with Lincoln and William Seward, his secretary of state.

The Confederates asked Lincoln for an armistice—a pause in the fighting—during which they could negotiate a truce, but Lincoln refused. He said that the only way to end the war was for the South to stop fighting and agree to rejoin the Union. The meeting, called the Hampton Roads Conference, was a failure from the Confederate perspective. The South, which had lost more men than it could replace and was miserably short of food and other supplies, would have to go on fighting.

Following the war's end, Stephens was arrested at his home, Liberty Hall, in Crawfordsville, Georgia, on May 11, 1865. He was imprisoned in Boston for several months. In 1866, he was elected to the United States Senate from Georgia but was not allowed to serve because of his role in the Confederacy, so he spent the next few years writing about the Confederacy and the war.

By 1873, Stephens was allowed to fill a vacancy in the United States House of Representatives, where he served until 1882. He resigned to become governor of Georgia, but he died after only four months in office.

▷ Judah Benjamin

Considered the most important figure in Jefferson Davis's cabinet and often referred to as "the brains of the Confederacy," Judah Benjamin served the Confederate States of America in its short life in three important roles: He was its attorney general, secretary of war, and secretary of state, in that order. Benjamin was born in 1811 in the Virgin Islands to Jewish parents who moved to North Carolina and then settled in Charleston, South Carolina. A brilliant child, he attended Yale Law School at age fourteen but left in his junior year. He moved to New Orleans and, among other things, taught English and

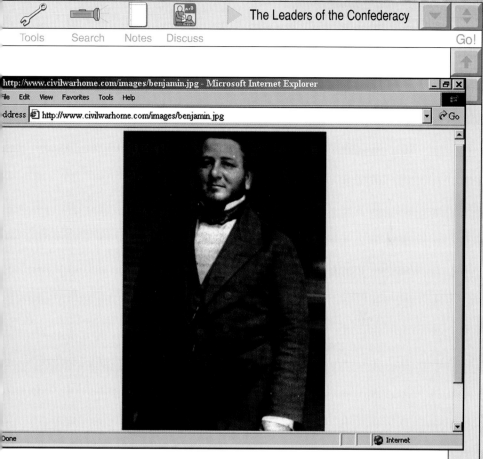

http://www.civilwarhome.com/images/benjamin.jpg - Microsoft Internet Explorer

File Edit View Favorites Tools Help

Address http://www.civilwarhome.com/images/benjamin.jpg Go

Done Internet

▲ *Judah Benjamin served in the Confederate cabinet in three capacities.*

studied French and the law. He was admitted to the bar in 1832 and became a prominent lawyer and a wealthy man, rich enough to buy a sugar plantation. He served in Louisiana's state legislature before being elected to the United States Senate in 1852 and reelected in 1858.

In December 1860, following South Carolina's secession, Benjamin delivered an address to the Senate that is often considered one of the best defenses of Southern policy. Benjamin resigned his Senate seat on February 4, 1861, following Louisiana's secession from the Union.

In the government of the Confederacy, Judah Benjamin first served as attorney general. In November

1861, he was appointed secretary of war. In that position, he was criticized for Confederate losses in the early years, especially Roanoke Island in North Carolina, which fell into Union hands in 1862. As Jefferson Davis's loyal secretary, Benjamin had to shoulder the blame, although many historians consider that blame unjustified because the Southern army lacked both the men and supplies of the Union army throughout the war. From March 1862 until the end of the war, Benjamin was the Confederacy's secretary of state. He had the difficult job of trying to persuade Great Britain and France to recognize the Confederacy. Had that recognition come, it would have brought much-needed help to a South that lacked industry and could really only provide the barest supplies for its troops. A Union victory at Sharpsburg (Antietam) in September 1862 and Lincoln's announcement of the Emancipation Proclamation, which would go into effect January 1, 1863, ended any chance that Europe would recognize the Confederacy, now that the issue of slavery was brought to the forefront.

Near the end of the war, with much of the South starving and in ruins and its army depleted and worn out, Benjamin quietly convinced Robert E. Lee and some other Confederate military leaders that the South's best chance to survive was to use slaves who were willing to fight for the Confederate army if they were promised freedom. But his idea was rejected by other members of the Confederacy. With the South's defeat, Benjamin escaped through Florida and the West Indies to Great Britain, where he established a successful law career once again. That escape was necessary because both Jefferson Davis and Judah Benjamin were suspected of having been

Tools   Search   Notes   Discuss   Go!

behind John Wilkes Booth's assassination of Abraham Lincoln, although neither had been involved in it.

John Slidell

John Slidell was born in New York City in 1793 but became a prominent Louisiana politician in the years leading up to the Civil War. He was a businessman and lawyer who moved to New Orleans in 1819 after his business failed during the War of 1812.

Slidell ran for Congress in 1828 and was defeated but was elected to the House of Representatives in 1843. He was a Louisiana Democrat who supported states'

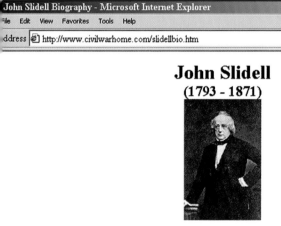

John Slidell Biography - Microsoft Internet Explorer

File   Edit   View   Favorites   Tools   Help

ddress   http://www.civilwarhome.com/slidellbio.htm   Go

John Slidell
(1793 - 1871)

Born in New York City, N.Y., 1793, the Northern-born Slidell rose to prominence as a Louisiana politician in the decades before the Civil War. A lawyer who began his career as a businessman, he moved to New Orleans in 1819 after his mercantile interests failed during the War of 1812.

Slidell lost a bid for Congress in 1828 and was frustrated in his political ambitions until 1843, when he was elected to the U.S. House of Representatives. As a states-rights Democrat he supported James K. Polk for the presidency in 1844 and used questionable legal means to assure him a Louisiana majority in the presidential election. Polk appointed Slidell commissioner to Mexico, with

Done   Internet

Though born in New York City, John Slidell was a states' rights Democrat whose service to the Confederacy positioned him in France for much of the war.

rights. He was then elected to the Senate in 1853. He and other congressmen from the South pushed for the Kansas-Nebraska Act in 1854, which dealt a blow to the limits of slavery's expansion that had been set by the Missouri Compromise in 1820. Slidell remained in favor of preserving the Union until Abraham Lincoln was elected president in 1860.

During the war, Slidell was appointed to represent the Confederacy as a diplomat in France, seeking much-needed aid from that country. He and fellow diplomat James Mason became involved in the *Trent* Affair when they were removed from the British ship they were on by the captain of a federal vessel. After protests by Great Britain and the Confederacy, the men were released and finally arrived in France, where they found the French sympathetic to the Confederate cause but unwilling to provide military aid to the Confederacy. Slidell remained in France throughout the war, and he did manage to arrange some Confederate financing through private French interests. But he was not able to secure the more considerable resources of the French government. He and his family stayed in Europe after the war, fearing that it was unsafe to return to the United States. He died in London, England, in 1871.

The Confederacy's Leading Generals

Robert Edward Lee was born in Westmoreland County, Virginia, on January 19, 1807, the son of Henry "Light Horse Harry" Lee, a heroic figure in America's fight for independence. In 1829, Lee graduated second in his class at West Point, and in four years at the academy, he did not earn a single demerit, which was considered a remarkable achievement. In 1831, Robert E. Lee married Mary Anne Randolph Custis, a great-granddaughter of Martha Washington. After serving on several important engineering projects, Lee fought with distinction under General Winfield Scott in the Mexican-American War. In 1852, Lee was appointed superintendent of the United States Military Academy at West Point and served in that position for three years. He was then posted to frontier duty in Texas until 1861.

Lee happened to be in Washington, D.C.,

General Robert E. Lee and his men survey the field of battle at Fredericksburg, December 1862.

when John Brown seized the Federal Arsenal at Harpers Ferry, then in Virginia, in 1859. Lee was sent to command the Marine detachment there and ordered Brown taken by force. He then returned to duty in Texas.

In April 1861, following Virginia's secession from the Union, Lee resigned from the United States Army and accepted command of Virginia's armed forces. He became a military adviser to President Jefferson Davis and was made a Confederate general. He organized Virginia's army before it was absorbed by the Confederacy. He was sent to organize defenses along the South Atlantic coast before Davis recalled him to Richmond early in 1862.

When Confederate general Joseph E. Johnston was wounded in the Battle of Seven Pines (or Fair Oaks), in Virginia in June 1862, Lee took over the command of the Army of Northern Virginia. Within a month, Lee attacked Union general George McClellan's Army of the Potomac during the Seven Days' Battles. Lee's forces drove the Union forces from their positions, which were threatening the Confederate capital. As a result of this move, Lee became an instant hero in the South.

Next, Lee defeated Union general John Pope's forces at the Second Battle of Manassas, August 29–30, 1862. But Lee's first Northern invasion was stopped at Sharpsburg, Maryland, in September 1862 by McClellan's forces. McClellan failed to pursue Lee, however, and he was able to retreat back to Virginia. The Battle of Sharpsburg was the bloodiest single day of fighting in the war, and the Confederacy suffered more than ten thousand casualties.

Lee's army then staged victories in Virginia over the Union army led by Ambrose Burnside and Joseph Hooker at the battles of Fredericksburg in December 1862 and

Chancellorsville in May 1863. To Lee's great sorrow, however, he lost his best general, Thomas "Stonewall" Jackson, at Chancellorsville.

Lee then attempted his second invasion of the North in the summer of 1863, to draw Union troops out of Virginia and give its farmers a chance to harvest their crops. But that attempt ended in a crushing defeat at the Battle of Gettysburg, Pennsylvania, July 1–3, 1863. Some historians blame Lee's defeat at Gettysburg on the failures of the men under him, particularly General James Longstreet. Other historians argue that Lee underestimated the size of the Northern forces that opposed him.

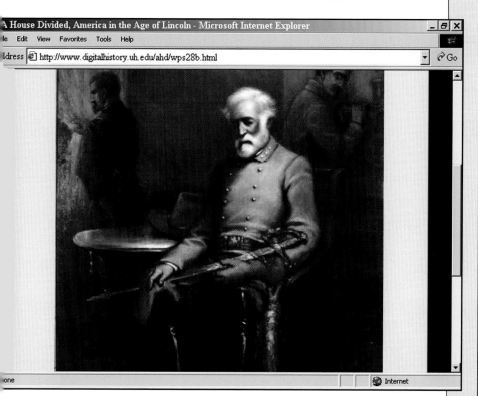

A House Divided, America in the Age of Lincoln - Microsoft Internet Explorer

File Edit View Favorites Tools Help

Address http://www.digitalhistory.uh.edu/ahd/wps28b.html   Go

Internet

▲ This Thomas Nast portrait of Robert E. Lee, waiting to surrender to Ulysses S. Grant at Appomattox Court House, paints the Confederate general as noble in defeat.

Lee himself assumed full blame for the loss at Gettysburg and offered his resignation to President Jefferson Davis, but Davis refused it.

Lee's next major campaign came against Ulysses S. Grant's troops in May 1864 during the Battle of the Wilderness. Grant was on the offensive, and Lee was able to slow his advance, but Lee's forces were not strong enough to turn back the much larger Union army. In July, Grant began the long siege of Petersburg, Virginia, outside the Confederate capital. That siege lasted until April 2, 1865, when Union troops finally broke through the Confederate defenses, and Lee was forced to retreat. A week later, with his forces severely depleted and not wanting to suffer further casualties, Robert E. Lee surrendered his Army of Northern Virginia to Ulysses S. Grant at Appomattox Court House, Virginia.

After the war, Lee served as president of Washington College, now named Washington and Lee University. Although Lee never received the official amnesty from President Andrew Johnson that he hoped for, he urged the people of the South to work toward peace and reconciliation following the war.

Some historians consider Robert E. Lee to have been the greatest general of the Civil War, citing Lee's military genius in keeping the Confederacy alive despite a lack of men and supplies. Others fault Lee for not having had an overall strategy to win the war.

Whichever viewpoint is correct, Robert E. Lee remains one of the South's most-beloved heroes, a gentle-man-soldier who also earned the respect of the people of the North.

▶ Thomas Jonathan "Stonewall" Jackson

Thomas Jonathan Jackson was the most respected Southern general of the Civil War after Robert E. Lee. Jackson graduated from West Point and served in the artillery during the Mexican-American War. He resigned from the army to become a professor at the Virginia Military Institute.

When the Civil War began, Jackson was commissioned a colonel in the Virginia army, and he first worked with recruits at Harpers Ferry. Then he took a brigade to Manassas, where he fought in the First Battle of Manassas, along with Joseph E. Johnston and P.G.T. Beauregard. It was in this battle that Jackson earned his nickname, Stonewall. Confederate general Barnard Bee is said to have urged his men on in battle by pointing to Jackson and saying, "There is Jackson standing like a stone wall! Rally behind the Virginians!"[1] That fall, Jackson was promoted in rank to major general.

During the winter, Jackson was involved in a futile campaign in the

Thomas Jonathan "Stonewall" Jackson was the most beloved Southern general after Robert E. Lee and remains a legendary figure in the South.

western part of Virginia that resulted in a long feud with General William Loring. Jackson submitted his resignation, but was talked out of it. He won several victories before joining Lee in defending Richmond.

General Jackson then commanded troops at the Second Battle of Manassas in August and in the invasion of Maryland at the Battle of Sharpsburg in September 1862. In May 1863, Jackson fought his greatest—and last—battle. His men struck the Union forces from behind near Chancellorsville, Virginia. The enemy forces were driven back in disorder. On the evening of May 2, Jackson rode out to scout the Union position when some of his men mistook him for the enemy and shot him.

Jackson was moved to a field hospital, where his left arm had to be amputated. Lee commented, "He has lost his left arm, but I have lost my right [arm]," referring to his trusted officer.[2] Already weakened, Jackson contracted pneumonia and died on May 10. His death was a great loss for the Confederate army and a great personal loss for Robert E. Lee.

Thomas Jonathan "Stonewall" Jackson had been a very religious man. Earlier, when asked how he stayed so cool in the midst of battle, he had replied, ". . . My religious belief teaches me to feel as safe in battle as in bed. God has fixed the time for my death. I do not concern myself about that. . . ."[3]

▷ James Ewell Brown Stuart

James Ewell Brown Stuart, known as Jeb, was born in Virginia in 1833. One of the most famous cavalrymen of the Civil War, he graduated from West Point and was sent to Kansas where he saw action against American Indians on the Plains. He later took part in subduing fights in

ttp://www.historyplace.com/civilwar/cwar-pix/chancellors1.jpg - Microsoft Internet Explorer

Edit View Favorites Tools Help

iress   http://www.historyplace.com/civilwar/cwar-pix/chancellors1.jpg   Go

ne   Internet

▲ *Confederate casualties line the Sunken Road after the Battle of Chancellorsville, May 1 to 4, 1863. Although a Confederate victory, Chancellorsville also proved to be a great loss for the Confederacy with the death of Stonewall Jackson.*

"Bleeding Kansas" between proslavery and antislavery forces in the territory.

In 1859, Stuart was the courier sent to deliver orders to Robert E. Lee to proceed to Harpers Ferry and capture John Brown, who had taken over the federal arsenal there with the aim to arm slaves in a rebellion. Stuart talked Lee into making him his aide-de-camp, or assistant, and Lee had him read the ultimatum to Brown to surrender or be fired upon. Stuart led the Marine assault on Brown, who was captured and later hanged for treason.

On April 22, 1861, a week after the attack on Fort Sumter, Stuart was promoted to captain in the United States Army. But since his home state of Virginia had already seceded from the Union, Stuart resigned from the army on May 14 and was made a lieutenant colonel of the Virginia infantry.

Stuart led a regiment at First Manassas and took part in the pursuit of the retreating Union army. He led his men on raids behind the Union lines. They did not do a lot of damage, but they made the Union army nervous and helped to boost the morale of the Confederate army.

Wearing a cloak and sporting a hat with a large plume, Stuart was a colorful figure on the battlefield. He lost his cloak and plume in the Second Battle of Manassas, but overran General John Pope's headquarters there. He grabbed Pope's dress uniform as well as papers that revealed Pope's plans, which proved to be a great asset to General Robert E. Lee in planning his strategy. As 1862 drew to a close, Stuart led a raid north of the Rappahannock River,

General Jeb Stuart, famous for his raids behind Union lines, was one of the most accomplished cavalrymen of the Civil War.

which resulted in more than two hundred Union casualties while the Confederacy suffered fewer than thirty.

At Chancellorsville, after Stonewall Jackson had been wounded, Stuart took command of Jackson's corps and led two charges against the enemy the next day. When the Battle of Gettysburg began in July 1863, Stuart was engaged in circling the Union army, depriving Lee of important information he needed at the time. Stuart arrived the second day of the battle and covered Lee's retreat to Virginia.

In May 1864, Stuart intercepted Union general Philip Sheridan's cavalry at Yellow Tavern, outside Richmond. Stuart's men were outnumbered, and he was wounded in the battle. He was taken to Richmond where he died the next day. Stuart, like Stonewall Jackson before him, died a legendary hero of the South.

Albert Sidney Johnston

Albert Sidney Johnston, born in Washington, Kentucky, in 1803, was considered by many in both the North and the South as one of the finest generals in the country in 1861. After his graduation from West Point in 1826, he served in the United States Army for eight years, taking part in the Black Hawk War. He resigned in 1834 to take care of his wife, who was ill. After she died, Johnston joined the revolutionary forces in Texas who were fighting to free Texas from Mexico's rule. Johnston became the commander of Texas forces and was then made secretary of war for Texas when it was an independent republic.

Johnston reentered the United States Army in 1849 and served in Texas. He also led an expedition against Mormon settlers in Utah in 1857. He was stationed in California when the Civil War broke out. He resigned his

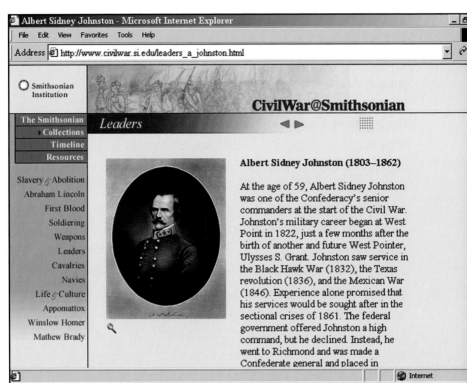

Albert Sidney Johnston - Microsoft Internet Explorer

File   Edit   View   Favorites   Tools   Help

Address   http://www.civilwar.si.edu/leaders_a_johnston.html

Smithsonian Institution

CivilWar@Smithsonian

Leaders

The Smithsonian
Collections
Timeline
Resources

Slavery & Abolition
Abraham Lincoln
First Blood
Soldiering
Weapons
Leaders
Cavalries
Navies
Life & Culture
Appomattox
Winslow Homer
Mathew Brady

Albert Sidney Johnston (1803–1862)

At the age of 59, Albert Sidney Johnston was one of the Confederacy's senior commanders at the start of the Civil War. Johnston's military career began at West Point in 1822, just a few months after the birth of another and future West Pointer, Ulysses S. Grant. Johnston saw service in the Black Hawk War (1832), the Texas revolution (1836), and the Mexican War (1846). Experience alone promised that his services would be sought after in the sectional crises of 1861. The federal government offered Johnston a high command, but he declined. Instead, he went to Richmond and was made a Confederate general and placed in

Internet

General Albert Sidney Johnston, highly regarded by his commander-in-chief, Jefferson Davis, was fifty-eight years old when the Civil War began. He would not live to see his sixtieth birthday, however—he was fatally wounded at Shiloh in 1862.

commission after Texas seceded in April 1861, but ever the loyal officer, he waited for his replacement to arrive in California before going to Richmond. Johnston was a close friend of Jefferson Davis. The president of the Confederacy said of him, "I hoped and expected that I had others who would prove generals, but I knew I had one, and that was Sidney Johnston."[4]

Davis put Johnston in charge of the western theater of operations. His troops were limited, but he established a line of defense that stretched across Kentucky. He held that line until the Union army broke through at Mill Springs in January 1862 and took Forts Henry and Donelson on the Tennessee River the next month. Johnston and his troops were forced to retreat into northern Mississippi.

He regrouped his men and in early April launched a surprise attack on Grant's army at Shiloh, in Tennessee. "We must this day conquer or perish," he said to one of the soldiers as they began battle.[5] While driving the enemy back, Johnston suffered a leg wound that he did not consider serious, but he had severed an artery, and he bled to death before his men realized that their commander was dying.

In a special message to the Confederate Congress, Jefferson Davis announced Johnston's death with great sadness: "Without doing injustice to the living, it may safely be said that our loss is irreparable. In his death, he has illustrated the character for which through life he was conspicuous—that of singleness of purpose and devotion to duty with his whole energies."[6]

James Longstreet

James Longstreet, born in South Carolina in 1821, spent his early years in Georgia and lived for a time in Alabama. Longstreet graduated from West Point in 1842 and fought in the Mexican-American War, where he was wounded at the Battle of Chapultepec. He resigned his commission in the United States Army in June 1861 to join the Confederate army, where he was surprised to be commissioned a colonel, since he had been a major in the United States Army.

By the time Longstreet fought in the First Battle of Manassas, he had been promoted to brigadier general. His reputation for courage and calm under fire helped him

to rise through the ranks of the Confederate army. Longstreet became a trusted friend to Robert E. Lee, and when Lee reorganized the Army of Northern Virginia, he gave Longstreet command of its First Corps.

From June to December 1862, Longstreet proved to be a capable subordinate to Robert E. Lee in Virginia during the Seven Days and Second Manassas campaigns as well as in the battles at Sharpsburg and Fredericksburg. But in June 1863, Longstreet offered a battle plan to Lee that would have protected strategic points in the West, including the vital Mississippi River port of Vicksburg.

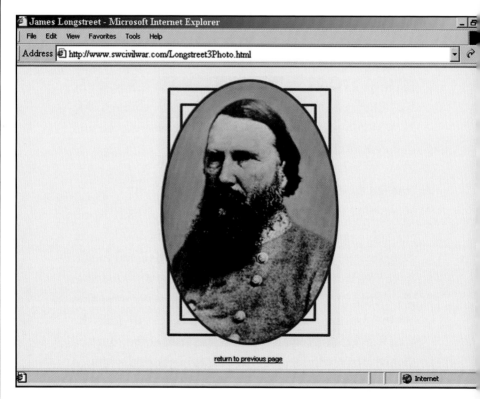

James Longstreet - Microsoft Internet Explorer

File   Edit   View   Favorites   Tools   Help

Address http://www.swcivilwar.com/Longstreet3Photo.html

return to previous page

Internet

General James Longstreet's reputation is still the subject of debate in the South. He committed two unpardonable sins: He criticized Robert E. Lee's strategy, and he joined the ranks of the Republican party following the war.

Lee instead chose to invade the North, to give Virginia farmers a chance to bring in their crops and to draw Federal forces away from other parts of the Confederacy. In the Battle of Gettysburg, fought in the fields of southern Pennsylvania from July 1 to 3, 1863, the Confederate army suffered more than 28,000 casualties. Longstreet's delay in taking the offensive at Gettysburg is considered by many historians to have cost Lee a victory there. Lee himself, however, never criticized Longstreet.

Following the devastating defeat at Gettysburg, Lee and the Confederacy's officials in Richmond decided to heed Longstreet's warning about the need to reinforce the West, but it was already too late for Vicksburg. Ulysses S. Grant had captured the city the day after the Battle of Gettysburg ended, and Confederate general Braxton Bragg's forces had been pushed into northern Georgia. Longstreet was sent to Georgia to reinforce Bragg's position, and his bravery in the Battle of Chickamauga against Union general George Thomas, September 18 to 20, was said to have inspired his men and fellow officers. In November and December, his seventeen-day siege at Knoxville against Ambrose Burnside's forces was far less successful, however. On the first day, Longstreet lost eight hundred men in only twenty minutes, and he was finally forced to retreat when Union general William Tecumseh Sherman approached with 25,000 men.

When Longstreet rejoined Lee's army at the Battle of the Wilderness outside Fredericksburg, Virginia, in May 1864, he was mistakenly shot by his own men—just as Stonewall Jackson had been shot in nearly the same area a year earlier. That injury prevented Longstreet from rejoining the Army of Northern Virginia until October,

during the siege of Petersburg. Longstreet remained with Lee through the surrender at Appomattox.

Following the war, Longstreet settled in New Orleans, became a Republican, and went on to serve in Ulysses S. Grant's administration as minister to Turkey. He wrote a book, *From Manassas to Appomattox*, in which he expressed his opinions of the war, which included a criticism of Lee's battle plan at Gettysburg. To most Southerners, these acts were unpardonable sins, and some former Confederate generals bitterly attacked Longstreet, questioning his loyalty to the Confederate cause. But to

▲ *Private Edwin Jennison of the Second Louisiana Regiment was neither a famous general nor a Southern leader. He was one of the hundreds of thousands of Confederate soldiers to lose his life in the Civil War when he was killed at Malvern Hill in July 1862.*

many of the men who had served under him—and even
to some of those who had served opposite—his reputation
as an excellent combat officer was untarnished.

Joseph Eggleston Johnston

Joseph Eggleston Johnston, born in Prince Edward
County, Virginia, in 1807, was the highest-ranking regu-
lar army officer to resign from the United States Army
and join the Confederacy. Some considered him a more
capable general than Robert E. Lee—Johnston himself
certainly thought so.

A West Point graduate, Johnston fought in the
Seminole Wars in Florida and in the Mexican-American
War. He was wounded in action in both wars.

At the outbreak of the Civil War, Johnston, a brigadier
general, resigned from the United States Army, where he
had served as the army's quartermaster general, in charge
of supplies. President Jefferson Davis made him a
brigadier general in the Confederate army in May 1861
and put him in charge of the command at Harpers Ferry.
In the First Battle of Manassas, Johnston's actions in coming to the aid of General P.G.T. Beauregard and his part
in the Confederate victory led him to be named general,
and he was given command of the Army of Northern
Virginia, which Jefferson Davis asked him to organize.
But Johnston felt that an attempt at reorganization would
be foolhardy at the time, and he ignored Davis's order.

There was a great deal of friction between Johnston
and Davis over the ranking of Confederate generals.
Johnston was ranked fourth, behind Samuel Cooper,
Albert Sidney Johnston, and Robert E. Lee. Since he had
been the highest-ranking officer to leave the Union army,
Joseph E. Johnston thought he should be ranked first in

the Confederate army. Throughout his career, he and Davis were at odds.

Johnston further irritated the Confederate president by withdrawing his army to a safer position after Manassas. He did keep Union general George McClellan from landing in the area of Urbanna, Virginia, but Johnston was blamed for the loss of a large number of Confederate supplies near Manassas when he withdrew.

In May 1862, outside Richmond, Joseph E. Johnston attacked the southern part of the Union army while it was divided by a rain-swollen river and was able to stop its advance. Johnston was severely wounded in the Battle of Seven Pines, however, and Robert E. Lee took over the defense of Richmond. Johnston referred to his injury and Lee's subsequent takeover by saying, "The shot that struck me down was the best ever fired for the

▲ *Joseph Eggleston Johnston's surrender to William Tecumseh Sherman in Greensboro, North Carolina, came nearly three weeks after Lee's surrender to Grant at Appomattox Court House, Virginia.*

Confederacy, for I possessed in no degree the confidence of the government, and now a man who does enjoy it will succeed me and be able to accomplish what I never could."[7] He realized that without the support of Jefferson Davis, with whom he was constantly at odds, he could never be an effective leader.

When Johnston recovered, he was sent west and given command of the western theater of operations. With limited troops, he and the Confederate army were defeated at Vicksburg, Mississippi, in July 1863, after a long siege by Ulysses S. Grant. Davis then ordered Johnston to go on the offensive against Union general William Tecumseh Sherman's army. But Johnston, then in command of the Army of the Tennessee, continued to fight defensively, since his forces were greatly outnumbered. Angered, Davis replaced him with General John Bell Hood, who fared no better against Sherman, but Johnston was given back his command in February 1865 by Robert E. Lee, then in charge of the Confederate armies.

Late in the war, Johnston was able to hinder Sherman's advance in North Carolina, but in order to save lives in a losing cause, Johnston surrendered to Sherman on April 26, 1865, against the wishes of Jefferson Davis.

After the war, Johnston worked in insurance and served from 1879 to 1881 in Congress as a representative from Virginia. In 1885, he was appointed federal commissioner of railroads by President Grover Cleveland. In his memoirs, he remained critical of the man he felt had thwarted his success in the war—the Confederate president, Jefferson Davis.

Chapter Notes

Chapter 1. Lee's Great Decision

1. Emory M. Thomas, *Robert E. Lee: A Biography* (New York: W.W. Norton & Co., 1995), p. 188.

2. Ibid., p. 189.

3. Walter Rawls, ed., *Great Civil War Heroes and Their Battles* (New York: Abbeville Press, 1985), p. 160.

Chapter 2. The Southern Perspective

1. United States Constitution, Amendment 10

Chapter 3. The Political Leaders of the Confederacy

1. William J. Cooper, Jr., *Jefferson Davis, American* (New York: Alfred A. Knopf, 2000), p. 26.

2. "Jefferson Davis Biography," *Civil War Home*, n.d., <http://www.civilwarhome.com/jdavisbio.htm> (December 30, 2003).

3. Ibid., p. 2.

4. Cooper, p. 330.

Chapter 4. The Confederacy's Leading Generals

1. James M. McPherson, *Battle Cry of Freedom: The Civil War Era* (New York and Oxford: Oxford University Press, 1988), p. 342.

2. Emory M. Thomas, *Robert E. Lee: A Biography* (New York: W. W. Norton & Co., 1995), p. 287.

3. Walter Rawls, ed., *Great Civil War Heroes and Their Battles* (New York: Abbeville Press, 1985), p. 227.

4. "General Albert Sydney Johnston," *The American Civil War*, n.d., <http://www.swcivilwar.com/asjohnston.html> (December 30, 2003).

5. Rawls, p. 233.

6. Ibid., p. 234.

7. "General Joseph Johnston," *The American Civil War*, n.d., <http://www.swcivilwar.com/jjohnston.html> (December 30, 2003).

Further Reading

Archer, Jules. *A House Divided: The Lives of Ulysses S. Grant and Robert E. Lee.* New York: Scholastic, 1995.

Collier, Christopher, and James Lincoln Collier. *Slavery and the Coming of the Civil War, 1831–1861.* New York: Benchmark Books, 2000.

Fradin, Dennis Brindell. *Bound for the North Star: True Stories of Fugitive Slaves.* New York : Clarion Books, 2000.

Gaines, Anne Graham. *The Confederacy and the Civil War.* Berkeley Heights, N.J.: Enslow Publishers, Inc., 2000.

Grabowski, Patricia A. *Robert E. Lee: Confederate General.* Philadelphia: Chelsea House Publishers, 2000.

Green, Carl R., and William R. Sanford. *Confederate Generals of the Civil War.* Springfield, N.J.: Enslow Publishers, Inc., 1998.

Gunderson, Cory Gideon. *Jefferson Davis.* Mankato, Minn.: Bridgestone Books, 2002.

Le Tourneau, Melanie. *James Longstreet.* Woodbridge, Conn.: Blackbirch Press, 2002.

Marrin, Albert. *Commander in Chief Abraham Lincoln and the Civil War.* New York: Dutton Children's Books, 1997.

McPherson, James M. *The Boys in Blue and Gray.* New York: Atheneum Books for Young Readers, 2002.

O'Connell, Kim A. *Major Battles of the Civil War.* Berkeley Heights, N.J.: Enslow Publishers, Inc., 2004.

Robertson, James I., Jr. *Standing Like a Stone Wall: The Life of General Thomas J. Jackson.* New York: Atheneum Books for Young Readers, 2001.

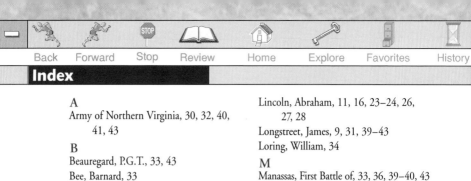
A
Army of Northern Virginia, 30, 32, 40, 41, 43

B
Beauregard, P.G.T., 33, 43
Bee, Barnard, 33
Benjamin, Judah, 9, 24–27
Black Hawk War, 18, 37
Blair, Francis, 11
Bragg, Braxton, 41
Brown, John, 30, 35
Burnside, Ambrose, 30, 41

C
Cameron, Simon, 11
Chancellorsville, Battle of, 31, 34, 37
Chickamauga, Battle of, 41
Cleveland, Grover, 45
Confederate States of America, 16, 17, 20–22, 22–24, 25–28, 29–45

D
Davis, Jefferson, 9, 17–22, 23–24, 26, 30, 32, 38, 39, 43, 44, 45
Davis, Sallie Knox Taylor, 19
Davis, Varina Howell, 19

F
Fredericksburg, Battle of, 30, 40

G
Gettysburg, Battle of, 31–32, 41, 42
Grant, Ulysses S., 32, 41, 42, 45

H
Hampton Roads Conference, 24
Hood, John Bell, 45
Hooker, Joseph, 30

J
Jackson, Thomas Jonathan "Stonewall," 9, 31, 33–34, 37
Johnson, Andrew, 22, 32
Johnston, Albert Sidney, 9, 37–39
Johnston, Joseph Eggleston., 9, 30, 33, 43–45

L
Lee, Henry "Light Horse" Harry, 29
Lee, Mary Ann Randolph Custis, 29
Lee, Robert Edward, 9, 10–12, 26, 29–32, 34, 35, 40, 43, 45
Letcher, John, 11

Lincoln, Abraham, 11, 16, 23–24, 26, 27, 28
Longstreet, James, 9, 31, 39–43
Loring, William, 34

M
Manassas, First Battle of, 33, 36, 39–40, 43
Manassas, Second Battle of, 30, 34, 36, 40
McClellan, George, 30, 44
Mexican-American War, 10, 19, 29, 33, 39
Monroe, James, 18

P
Petersburg, siege of, 32, 42
Pierce, Franklin, 20
Pope, John, 30, 36

R
Richmond, Virginia, 18, 37

S
Scott, Winfield, 10–11
Seminole Wars, 43
Seven Days' Battles, 30
Seven Pines (Fair Oaks), Battle of, 30
Seward, William, 23
Sharpsburg (Antietam), Battle of, 26, 30, 34, 40
Sheridan, Philip, 37
Sherman, William Tecumseh, 41, 45
Shiloh, Battle of, 39
slavery, 14
Slidell, John, 9, 27–28
states' rights, 14–16, 19, 27–28
Stephens, Alexander Hamilton, 9, 22–24
Stuart, James Ewell Brown "Jeb," 9, 34–37

T
Taylor, Zachary, 19
Thomas, George, 41
Trent Affair, 28

U
United States Constitution, 15
United States Military Academy (West Point), 18, 29, 33, 34, 37, 39, 43

V
Vicksburg, siege of, 41, 45

W
Washington, Martha, 29
Washington and Lee University (Washington College), 32
Wilderness, Battle of the, 32, 41